I0015999

TABLE OF CONTENTS

Introduction 4

Step #1: Choose Your Platform(s) 8

Step #2: Optimize Your Social Media Profile 13

    1. Select A Professional Username 15

    2. Use A High-Quality Profile Photo 16

    3. Write A Compelling "About" Section 17

    4. Upload A Professional Cover Photo 18

    5. Enter All Your Contact Information 19

    6. Be Professional 20

Step #3: Create A Posting Schedule 21

Step #4: Begin Posting On Social Media 26

Step #5: Engage With Your Followers 30

Step #6: Follow The Right People 35

Step #7: Use Hashtags 39

Step #8: Experiment 43

Don't Wait Any Longer! 44

INTRODUCTION

Facebook currently has over 2 billion daily active users. YouTube has almost 2 billion active users. Instagram has 1 billion. Twitter has approximately 330 million, LinkedIn has 303 million, and Pinterest has 250 million.

Why all these statistics about how many social media users there are?

To make one, powerful point: your customers and potential customers are DEFINITELY on at least one, if not more of these social media platforms.

With such a staggering number of people using social media every single day, it is one of the most POWERFUL ways to grow your business.

Social media platforms allow you to attract new customers and connect with audiences that you never would otherwise.

And if your business isn't location dependent, you can reach customers thousands of miles away through social media. You don't need to rely only on local customers. By posting on social media, you can even attract customers from other countries.

You can get your brand in front of a vast audience who might otherwise not hear of you. Through consistent posting on social media, you can build a powerful brand that separates you from the crowd.

And you can establish yourself as a thought leader in your industry by regularly posting new, insightful content.

Of course, these realities also raise some important questions:

- What is the best platform to use?
- What tactics should you use to be seen by the most people?

- Are there certain types of content that perform better than others?
- How can you regularly post content?
- What etiquette rules do you need to follow?

Many business owners think that if they simply start posting on social media, they'll be successful and attract new customers. But it doesn't work this way. In order to build your business through social media, you need to have a strategy in place.

You need to know where you're going to post, what you're going to post, how often you're going to post, and more. It's important to have a strategy for engaging with your audience. Simply put, you need to have a plan.

It's not enough to post across a variety of social media networks. Without a definitive plan for how you're going to use social media, you probably won't get the results that you want.

However, if you do have a plan, you'll find yourself quickly building an audience.

In this report, you'll find a step-by-step guide to social media strategy for building your business. We'll guide you through the what, why, and how, so that by the end, you have a firm plan in place.

Ready?

Let's dive in.

STEP #1:
Choose Your Platform(s)

The first, and perhaps most important step, is to choose the primary social media platforms you will focus on.

Instead of trying to post on every social media platform out there, focus on the one or two that will have the most impact on your business.

In order to do this, you need to know your audience:

- Where do they spend most of their time when it comes to social media?

- Where do they like to interact with brands and businesses?

- What sites influence them to purchase?

- Who are the biggest influencers in your space and what platforms do they use?

If your audience is younger, you may want to focus on Instagram and YouTube, which have a strong following among Millennials. If your focus is on business professionals, LinkedIn may be a good place to focus. If you're targeting women, Pinterest is probably a good place to start.

Think of it this way…

You want to be where your audience is.

You want to publish most of your content on the social media site where your audience hangs out the most. After all, you want your audience to interact with your content.

If you publish primarily on platforms where they don't spend their time, they'll never engage with what you post.

If you don't know where your audience spends most of their social media time, simply ask them!

Send out an email to your list and ask them to tell you what social media platforms they use the most. Create a poll on several different social media sites and ask your followers to respond.

Asking is one of the most effective ways to find out where your audience spends their time.

Another great way to determine where your audience spends their time is to look at the content you've already posted on social media and see what has gotten the biggest response.

Have you gotten more comments, likes, and shares on one particular social media site? That may be the one you want to focus on.

One other thing to consider when choosing your social media platform is what you're selling. Depending on the products or services you sell, one platform may be better than another.

For example, if you sell physical products, a visual platform like Instagram or Pinterest might be the best option for you.

On the other hand, if you're primarily focused on selling services, a platform like Facebook, Twitter, or LinkedIn might work more effectively for you since you can explain a bit more about what you're selling.

As you consider which platform(s) to use, it's essential that you think smaller rather than bigger. You don't want to spread yourself too thin across multiple social media platforms.

It would be better to focus on and master one or two platforms than to try to constantly post on ten different ones.

The reality is that you probably don't have enough time to post across a variety of platforms. You will get better results if you give 100% of your energy to a few platforms instead of 25% of your energies to a bunch of different platforms.

If you're still not sure which platform to focus on even after surveying your existing audience, you can always fall back on Facebook. With over 2 billion users, you can be sure that your target audience spends at least some time on the site.

At the end of the day, what matters most is not the particular platform you choose but rather that you choose one and stick with it. When it comes to social media, consistency is almost always the most effective way to win an audience.

So pick your platform and commit yourself to posting regularly on it.

STEP #2:
Optimize Your Social Media Profile

If you went to a business's social media page and saw that they didn't have a picture, barely had any information about their business, and weren't very active, would you want to connect with that business? Probably not.

This is why it's essential that you optimize your social media profile. You want to make your profile as informative and attractive as possible. You want your profile to draw people in, not push them away.

As Itamar Gero says:

> Part of your lead generation effort involves building a strong social persona. Once your social profile is up, potential clients are likely going to come across it - and not just potential clients, but also anyone within their extended network.

The last thing you want is to have a social profile that's anything but presentable.

So how do you optimize your profile?

Here are some specific recommendations.

1. Select A Professional Username

Ideally, you want your username to be either your name or the name of your company. In other words, you don't want to create a username like TulipGirl997. This comes across as unprofessional and won't set you up for success.

Your username typically is also the URL of your social profile. For example, if your username is JohnSmith, your Facebook profile URL will be www.facebook.com/JohnSmith.

Ideally, you want to keep your username the same across all the social networks. This helps people find you on every social platform.

For Facebook, set up a professional page, not just a personal profile. In other words, set up a page that is dedicated solely to your business. You will only be posting business related things on this page. No photos of your pets, memes, or other unrelated items. You want to use your business page to build your brand.

2. Use A High-Quality Profile Photo

Whether you're uploading a picture of yourself or your logo, use a high-quality photo. Ideally, the photo will have been professionally taken or the logo professionally designed.

The photo is one of the first things that people see when they click on your social media profile. You want to put your best foot forward when it comes to your profile photo.

If you need to have a logo designed, Fiverr and Upwork are great places to start. They make it incredibly easy to get a logo designed inexpensively.

3. Write A Compelling "About" Section

This section is where you tell the story of your business. It's where you communicate what you're all about and what matters most to you. Make your About section both compelling and concise.

Depending on the social platform you use, you may have limited space to write your about information. In that case, try to get to the heart of what makes your business different from every other business.

What is it that you do that sets you apart from everyone else? Include that information in your About section.

Also include links to your website, your other social media profiles, and any other relevant links. Make your About section as thorough as possible so that people get a good feel for what your business is all about.

4. Upload A Professional Cover Photo

Almost every social media platform allows you to upload a cover photo. The cover photo spans the top of your social media profile and sits behind your profile photo. Like your profile photo, you want your cover photo to be as professional as possible.

If your business has a slogan or motto, consider putting that slogan on your cover photo. If you don't have a slogan, you could feature a photo of your products. Ideally, you want your cover photo to further emphasize some element of your business.

On some social media sites, such as Facebook, you can upload a cover video instead of a photo. In the video, you can highlight unique aspects of your business.

5. Enter All Your Contact Information

Remember, you're trying to grow your business using social media. This means you want to make it as easy as possible for potential customers to contact you. In the Contact section, include as many possible ways to contact you as possible.

This can include your business phone number, email address, physical address, and any other possible ways of contact.

You can also invite people to message you directly on the platform.

6. Be Professional

As you optimize your overall profile, think about how you want to represent yourself and your business online. Your social media profile will be the first touch point for some potential clients, and it's critical that your profile feel professional.

If your social media profile isn't optimized and doesn't feel professional, there's a good chance you'll turn away potential clients.

STEP #3:
Create A Posting Schedule

Once you've optimized your social media profile, it's time to map out how often you'll be posting, as well as what you'll be posting.

Ideally, you want to do this before you actually begin posting on social media. This will help you map out exactly what you want to post.

Consider creating a social media calendar in which you map out what you will post each day during a given time period (week, month, year). This calendar will include what you're going to post, as well as when you'll post it.

When creating your social media calendar, ask yourself these questions:

- How often will you post? Ideally, post at least once per day. This will keep your social media profile active and show your followers that you're engaged on social media.

- What sort of content will you post? Your business will shape the types of content you share.

  For example, if you're a life coach, you may want to regularly share inspirational quotes and photos. If you're a health practitioner, daily health tips could be incredibly helpful for your audience.

  When it comes to determining the types of content you're going to post, think of what will add the most value to your audience.

- What formats will you use? The most effective businesses utilize a variety of formats on social media. In other words, they don't just post text. They also use images, videos, polls, quizzes, and more. The more variety you use, the more you'll appeal to a wide range of individuals.

If you're struggling to figure out what to post, you may want to use a tool like this Social Media Calendar. This will give you inspiration for every day of the year. It will also guide you as to what types of content might be most relevant depending on the time of year (holidays, seasons, etc.).

You may be thinking: Why do I have to map all this out in advance? Why can't I just start posting?

There are two reasons why you should utilize a social media calendar. The first is that it helps you to be consistent with your posting. One of the biggest challenges that business owners face when using social media is being consistent.

If you're not consistent, you can lose the attention of your audience. After all, there are millions of things being posted every single day. If you're not consistently posting, your audience will turn their attention elsewhere.

Marianne Litman says it like this:

> If your social media goes dark for weeks at a time, you're not doing yourself or your followers any favors. Waiting weeks, or even days, between posts can kill off the enthusiasm you've built up. This can lead to an uninterested

audience or people jumping ship completely and unfollowing you.

Make a schedule that suits your workflow and keep it up. It could be that you have new work every Monday, Wednesday and Friday, or perhaps you post your best work from the week on Sunday mornings. It doesn't need to be a huge undertaking; it just needs to be consistent.

By creating a social media calendar, you do the hard work of figuring out what you're going to post up front. You take the guesswork away and ensure that you won't struggle to figure out what to publish.

This makes it much easier for you to be consistent over the long run since you don't have to constantly be trying to figure out what you're going to post.

Second, using a social media calendar "forces" you to be active on social media. You can't use the excuse of not knowing what to post. You've already laid out what you're going to post and it's important to stick to your schedule if you're going to win new customers.

STEP #4:
Begin Posting On Social Media

Once you've created your social media content calendar, it's time to begin posting on social media. This is where the rubber meets the road. It's time to start actually putting out valuable content on your chosen social media channels.

What sort of content should you be posting?

If you want to win new clients and satisfy your existing ones, it's essential to post content that will add value to your audience.

This is a critical point.

You're not just posting to post. Rather you're trying to provide your audience with high-value information that will help them live their best life possible.

Each post should be helpful in some way to your audience.

Your posts should help your audience:

- Think about something in a new way
- Take action like they never have
- Laugh or smile
- Learn something valuable

Again, this goes back to knowing your audience.

If you know your audience well, you know what they will find most valuable. If you don't know your audience, you'll struggle to post things that resonate with them.

Consider posting things like:

- Inspirational quotes
- Tips and tactics

- Tutorial videos
- Live videos
- Pictures that will motivate your audience
- And more

For example, let's say that you're a health and wellness coach. You could post:

- Inspirational quotes about being healthy
- Tips and tactics for eating healthier
- A tutorial video on how to perform a particular exercise
- A live video in which you answer questions from your audience
- Pictures of people performing challenging exercises

When creating your content calendar and posting on social media, constantly ask yourself the following question:

Is this adding value to my audience?

If it is, then post it. If you don't think it will add much value to your audience, then don't post it.

If you're not sure which types of content add the most value to your audience, try experimenting with different formats. You might find that videos perform better than photos, or that your audience really likes tutorials and tips.

Test out a variety of formats and see which ones resonate most with your audience.

You may be thinking: I don't have time to constantly be posting!

The good news is that you don't have to be on all the different social media platforms all day every day.

Using a tool like Buffer or Hootsuite, you can actually schedule out weeks, or even months, of posts in advance.

Consider using your social media calendar in conjunction with one of these tools. By scheduling a significant number of social media posts in advance, you can save yourself hours of time.

STEP #5:
Engage With Your Followers

It's not enough to simply post on social media and then go on your way.

The real power of social media is that it creates conversations between you and your followers. At least, it should create conversations. Conversations are the key to getting more clients through social media.

It's important to regularly, consistently engage with your followers by responding to comments, answering questions, solving challenges, and more.

Social media is not a one-way street. Rather, it's a conversation between you and those who follow you. A conversation involves both speaking (posting) and listening (responding).

If you want to build relationships and gain clients through social media, you need to be having conversations, not just publishing new content.

One of the things that matters most when it comes to social media is that you feel authentic. You don't want to come across as a huge corporation who only posts on social media and never engages in conversation. Instead, you want to authentically engage with your followers. Authenticity is attractive. It will attract new followers and turn them into new clients.

Another reason to engage with followers is that social media platforms tend to prioritize the posts with the most engagement. The posts with the most likes, comments, shares, and overall engagement get shown more frequently than those posts with very little engagement.

If you want to get your posts seen by as many people as possible, then you absolutely must engage with your followers on a regular basis.

You must:

- Talk with your followers
- Create conversations
- Answer questions
- Respond to any problems that are raised

Rather than talking at your audience, your goal is to talk with them and, as much as possible, create real relationships with them.
What are some ways that you can create conversations with your followers?

- Ask questions.
- Do live videos in which you talk directly with your audience.
- Conduct polls.

- Ask people to comment on a particular subject.
- Make statements that will get people talking (just be careful about being too controversial).
- And more

Focus on being as real and authentic as possible on social media and you're guaranteed to create conversations with your followers.

STEP #6:
Follow The Right People

Social media isn't just about getting people to follow you. It's also about following the right people and having conversations with them.

Consider following influencers in your industry.

For example, if you're a financial adviser, follow other financial advisers in your industry. If you're a life coach, try to connect with other life coaches. If you're in the health and wellness space, follow other health and wellness practitioners.

Once you've started following them, interact with the material they share online. Comment on it, repost it, and share it with your own followers. Try to develop relationships with others and simply be part of the conversation that's happening.

Additionally, consider being part of groups that are related to your industry. Both Facebook and LinkedIn have robust group features, and there are literally millions of groups about every subject imaginable.

- Join the groups.
- Engage in conversation.
- Try to help others.
- Be a useful resource.

One note of importance regarding groups. You must be very careful about promoting yourself and your services in groups. Many groups have strict rules about this kind of thing.

When you join a group, focus on adding value, not promoting yourself. The more value that you add, the more you'll become known as an expert in your industry. This will naturally attract clients to you.

As you follow influencers in your industry and take part in groups, take note of the valuable information that others are sharing. What sorts of posts do others share that resonate deeply with you? What content adds the most value to you?

Additionally, what sort of content seems to get the best response? What posts generate the most conversations and engagement?

This is the kind of content that you want to be sharing with your audience. You don't have to be completely original with what you share online. Don't be afraid to adopt techniques and strategies that are working well for others.

In addition to joining online groups, there are also several platforms that focus heavily on answering questions that are posed by users. For example, Quora lets any user post a question and then other users try to answer that question.

Quora is a great place to show off your expertise without being overly promotional.

It lets you speak directly to a person's challenges, offer helpful advice and answers, and build relationships online. If you do it right and add a large amount of value to those on the platform, it can certainly lead to more clients.

STEP #7:
Use Hashtags

Hashtags are words with the "#" symbol before them.

For example:

- #MondayMotivation
- #CrossfitLife
- #ChiropracticCare
- #Vegan

Hashtags are used as a way of grouping posts by subject. If you add a hashtag to a post, it will be grouped with all the other posts people have made using that hashtag.

If you see a post with a hashtag, you can click on that hashtag and see all the other posts with the same hashtag. For example, if you clicked on the hashtag #CrossfitLife, you would see all the other posts people had created about this topic if they used the #CrossfitLife hashtag.

Some sites, such as Twitter, highlight the most popular hashtags, giving you a sense of what's trending at any given time.

You can also follow hashtags so that you regularly see posts with a given hashtag.

The power of hashtags is that they allow you to get your content in front of a broader audience. In other words, you can have your posts seen by more than just your followers. By adding the appropriate hashtags, you can get them seen by thousands, if not millions of others.

How exactly do you use hashtags?

Typically, it works like this. You create a social media post. At the end of the post, you add a hashtag that is somehow related to the post. For example, let's say you're a health coach and you want to post a tip related to Crossfit workouts.

You would create your post, and then at the end, put your hashtag(s). It might look something like this:

> Before you do any Crossfit workout, spend at least ten minutes getting warmed up and stretched out. #Crossfit #CrossfitLife #CrossfitWorkout

Notice that you can add multiple hashtags to a post. Depending on the platform you're using, you may be limited by space in terms of how many hashtags are appropriate.

Generally speaking, you don't want hashtags to dominate the post. You want them to be toward the end of a post.

One thing to be careful about. If your hashtags aren't really related to the content of your post, there's a chance you could turn people away from you.

For example, if you attach a Crossfit hashtag to a completely unrelated post about a television show you like, some people won't like it and will feel like you're "abusing" hashtags.

As much as possible, keep your hashtags closely related to the content you're posting.

There are a number of websites that can help you find the right hashtags to use with your social media posts. These sites include:

- All Hashtag
- SeekMetrics
- Tailwind
- Ingramer

STEP #8:
Experiment

If you truly want to succeed on social media, you'll need to experiment to see what works best.

Different types of content will resonate with your audience. You may find that videos work really well while inspirational quotes don't perform as well. Or you may find that asking questions generates a lot of discussion, but polls fall flat.

Experimentation is especially critical since social media platforms are constantly changing.

Currently, Facebook gives preference to posts that keep people on their site, such as videos. These posts show up in people's news feeds more often. Facebook doesn't give nearly as much exposure to posts that send people off their website, such as links.

But this could change. In the future, Facebook may give preference to some other type of content.

The moral of the story?

Be constantly testing to see what works most effectively.

As you test, you'll discover what adds the most value to your audience. Then you can post more of this type of content, which will generate significantly more engagement.

It ends up being a virtuous cycle that helps you connect with more and more people on social media.

DON'T WAIT ANY LONGER!

If you're not regularly using social media to build your business, you should be. The advantages of using social media are enormous. With social media you can:

- Attract new clients
- Build your brand
- Establish yourself as a thought leader
- Connect with new audiences
- Create meaningful relationships
- Connect with other influencers
- And so much more

Thankfully, it's not particularly complicated to get started building your business through social media.

Simply follow the eight-step process we laid out:

1. Choose your platform.
2. Optimize your social media profile.
3. Create a posting schedule.
4. Start posting on social media.
5. Engage with your followers.
6. Follow the right people.
7. Use hashtags.
8. Experiment.

You don't need to be intimidated by social media. Even if you've never consistently posted on a platform, you can get started today. You can easily start building your business through the power of social media.

So, don't wait any longer. There are clients out there just waiting for you to find them.

EXCLUSIVE OFFER

You took action to take control of your income and future, and for that I want to give you an exclusive offer only available to those who purchase this book.

There is much work ahead to get your business launched, and I want to help you get there.

That is why I developed the Brand Awareness Accelerator Training, a step-by-step training course to help you get the attention of your target audience and position your business at the top of their minds.

Below is a coupon code for you to get 50% off this training.

BONUS: When you purchase the training using the code below, you will also receive a complimentary coaching call where I will help you set goals and milestones to ensure
your success.

Register at: getmindmagnet.com/register/p2p

Use Code: socialbook